PIANO · VOCAL · GUITAR

# TORCH SONGS

## A COLLECTION OF SULTRY JAZZ AND BIG BAND STANDARDS

ANGEL EYES · CRY ME A RIVER · I CAN'T GET STARTED · I GOT IT BAD AND THAT AIN'T GOOD · I'M GLAD THERE IS YOU · LOVER MAN (OH, WHERE CAN YOU BE?) · MISTY · MY FUNNY VALENTINE · STORMY WEATHER · AND MANY MORE!

ISBN 0-7935-0289-6

7777 W. BLUEMOUND RD. P.O. BOX 13819 MILWAUKEE, WI 53213

# C O N T

# E N T S

# CONTENTS

# AFTER YOU

Words and Music by
COLE PORTER

# ANGEL EYES

Words by EARL BRENT
Music by MATT DENNIS

# BABY, WON'T YOU PLEASE COME HOME

Words and Music by CHARLES WARFIELD
and CLARENCE WILLIAMS

# BLACK COFFEE

Words and Music by PAUL FRANCIS WEBSTER
and SONNY BURKE

# CAN'T HELP LOVIN' DAT MAN

Words by OSCAR HAMMERSTEIN II
Music by JEROME KERN

# COME RAIN OR COME SHINE

Words by JOHNNY MERCER
Music by HAROLD ARLEN

# CRY ME A RIVER

Words and Music by
ARTHUR HAMILTON

# DO NOTHIN' TILL YOU HEAR FROM ME

Words and Music by BOB RUSSELL
and DUKE ELLINGTON

# DON'T EXPLAIN

Words and Music by BILLIE HOLIDAY
and ARTHUR HERZOG

Hush now, don't ex - plain! Just say you'll re -

main, I'm glad you're back don't ex -

plain! _____ Qui - et, don't ex -

# THE END OF A LOVE AFFAIR

Words and Music by
EDWARD C. REDDING

# GET OUT OF TOWN

Words and Music by
COLE PORTER

44

so bit - ter sweet that, dar - ling, it's get - ting me down.

So on your mark, get set, get out of

town.

town.

# EVERYTHING HAPPENS TO ME

Words by TOM ADAIR
Music by MATT DENNIS

# GOD BLESS THE CHILD

Words and Music by ARTHUR HERZOG JR.
and BILLIE HOLIDAY

# GUESS WHO I SAW TODAY

Words and Music by MURRAY GRAND
and ELISSE BOYD

# A GOOD MAN IS HARD TO FIND

Words and Music by
EDDIE GREEN

Moderately

Verse

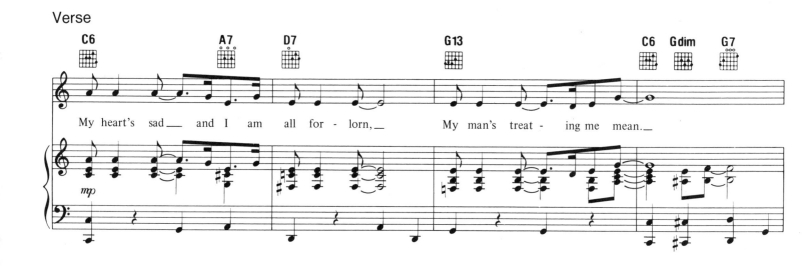

My heart's sad __ and I am all for-lorn, __ My man's treat - ing me mean. __

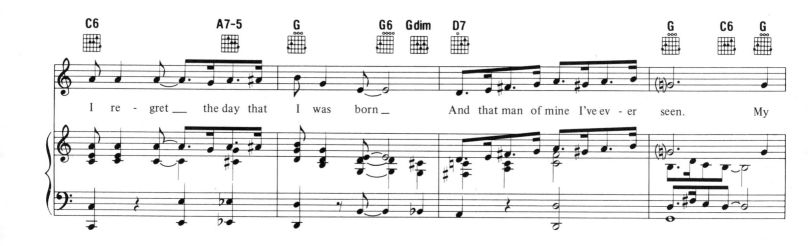

I re - gret __ the day that I was born __ And that man of mine I've ev - er seen. My

# HERE'S THAT RAINY DAY

Words and Music by JOHNNY BURKE
and JAMES VAN HEUSEN

# I CAN'T GET STARTED

Words by IRA GERSHWIN
Music by VERNON DUKE

# I CONCENTRATE ON YOU

Words and Music by
COLE PORTER

# I CRIED FOR YOU

Word and Music by ARTHUR FREED,
GUS ARNHEIM and ABE LYMAN

# (I Don't Stand)
# A GHOST OF A CHANCE
## (With You)

Words and Music by NED WASHINGTON,
BING CROSBY and VICTOR YOUNG

Moderately, Singable

# I GOT IT BAD AND THAT AIN'T GOOD

Words by PAUL FRANCIS WEBSTER
Music by DUKE ELLINGTON

# I SHOULD CARE

Words and Music by SAMMY CAHN,
AXEL STORDAHL and PAUL WESTON

# ILL WIND
## (You're Blowin' Me No Good)

Words by TED KOEHLER
Music by HAROLD ARLEN

# I'M GLAD THERE IS YOU
## (In This World Of Ordinary People)

Words and Music by PAUL MADEIRA
and JIMMY DORSEY

# I'LL BE AROUND

Words and Music by
ALEC WILDER

# LUSH LIFE

Words and Music by
BILLY STRAYHORN

# JUST FOR A THRILL

Words and Music by LIL ARMSTRONG
and DON RAYE

How could I poss-i-bly know? How could I have con-ceived it, that you'd try to hurt me so? I'd nev-er have be-lieved it. I was a fool, but you were

**MCA MUSIC PUBLISHING**

# LAZY AFTERNOON

Words by JOHN LATOUCHE
Music by JEROME MOROSS

# LITTLE GIRL BLUE

Words by LORENZ HART
Music by RICHARD RODGERS

Dm7 D7-9 Gm7 C7 F Bbmaj7 C9 F Ab
send a ten - der Blue boy to cheer a lit - tle girl blue?
G Gb F Gm7 C7 F
When I was ver - y young the world was young - er than
strung with ev - 'ry star in the
Am7 Ab7 Gm7 C7 F
I, As mer - ry as a car - ou - sel The cir - cus tent was
sky A - bove the ring I loved so well.
Dm7 Gm7 F
Now the young world has grown old, Gone are the
C7
tin - sel and gold.
D.S. al Coda
CODA
F Ab G Gb F
Blue?

# LOVER MAN
## (OH, WHERE CAN YOU BE?)

by JIMMY DAVIS, ROGER "RAM" RAMIREZ
and JIMMY SHERMAN

# MAD ABOUT THE BOY

Words and Music by
NOEL COWARD

mis - er - y and joy; _____ I'm feel - ing quite in - sane and young a - gain, and

all be - cause I'm mad a - bout the boy. _____

It seems a lit - tle sil - ly for a

# MAN IN A RAINCOAT

Words and Music by
WARWICK WEBSTER

# THE MAN THAT GOT AWAY

(From The Motion Picture "A STAR IS BORN")

Music by HAROLD ARLEN
Lyric by IRA GERSHWIN

# MAYBE THIS TIME

Lyric by FRED EBB
Music by JOHN KANDER

# MEAN TO ME

Words and Music by
FRED E. AHLERT and ROY TURK

# MIDNIGHT SUN

Word and Music by LIONEL HAMPTON,
SONNY BURKE and JOHNNY MERCER

Slowly, with a beat

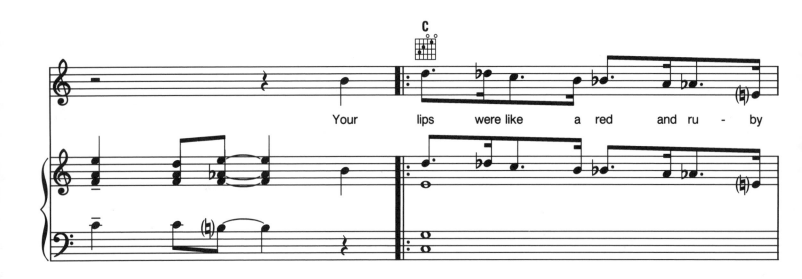

Your lips were like a red and ru - by

chal - ice, warm - er than the sum - mer night,

# MISTY

Words by JOHNNY BURKE
Music by EROLL GARNER

# MORE THAN YOU KNOW

Words by WILLIAM ROSE and EDWARD ELISCU
Music by VINCENT YOUMANS

Slowly, With Expression

# MY FOOLISH HEART

Words by NED WASHINGTON
Music by VICTOR YOUNG

Slowly and expressively

# MY FUNNY VALENTINE

## (From "BABES IN ARMS")

Words by LORENZ HART
Music by RICHARD RODGERS

# MY ONE AND ONLY LOVE

Words by ROBERT MELLIN
Music by GUY WOOD

# SOME OF THESE DAYS

Words and Music by
SHELTON BROOKS

# NO ORCHIDS FOR MY LADY

Words and Music by ALAN STRANKS
and JACK STRACHEY

# THE OTHER WOMAN

Words and Music by
JESSIE MAE ROBINSON

# THE PARTY'S OVER

Words by BETTY COMDEN & ADOLPH GREEN
Music by JULE STYNE

# SPRING CAN REALLY HANG YOU UP THE MOST

Lyric by FRAN LANDESMAN
Music by TOMMY WOLF

Once I was a sen-ti-ment-al thing,

threw my heart a-way each spring.

Now a spring ro-mance has-n't got a chance,

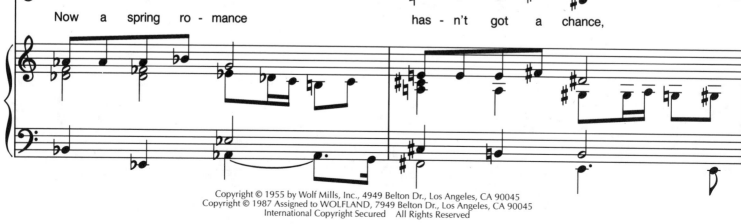

# STORMY WEATHER
# (KEEPS RAININ' ALL THE TIME)

Lyrics by TED KOEHLER
Music by HAROLD ARLEN

# A SUNDAY KIND OF LOVE

Words and Music by BARBARA BELLE, LOUIS PRIMA,
ANITA LEONARD and STAN RHODES

# THAT'S ALL

Words and Music by ALAN BRANDT
and BOB HAYMES

# THE THRILL IS GONE

Words by LEW BROWN
Music by RAY HENDERSON

# TRAVELIN' LIGHT

Words by SIDNEY CLARE
Music by HARRY AKST

# TROUBLE IN MIND

Words and Music by
RICHARD M. JONES

# WHEN THE SUN COMES OUT

Lyrics by TED KOEHLER
Music by HAROLD ARLEN

# WHY WAS I BORN

Words by OSCAR HAMMERSTEIN II
Music by JEROME KERN

# WILLOW WEEP FOR ME

Words and Music by
ANN RONELL

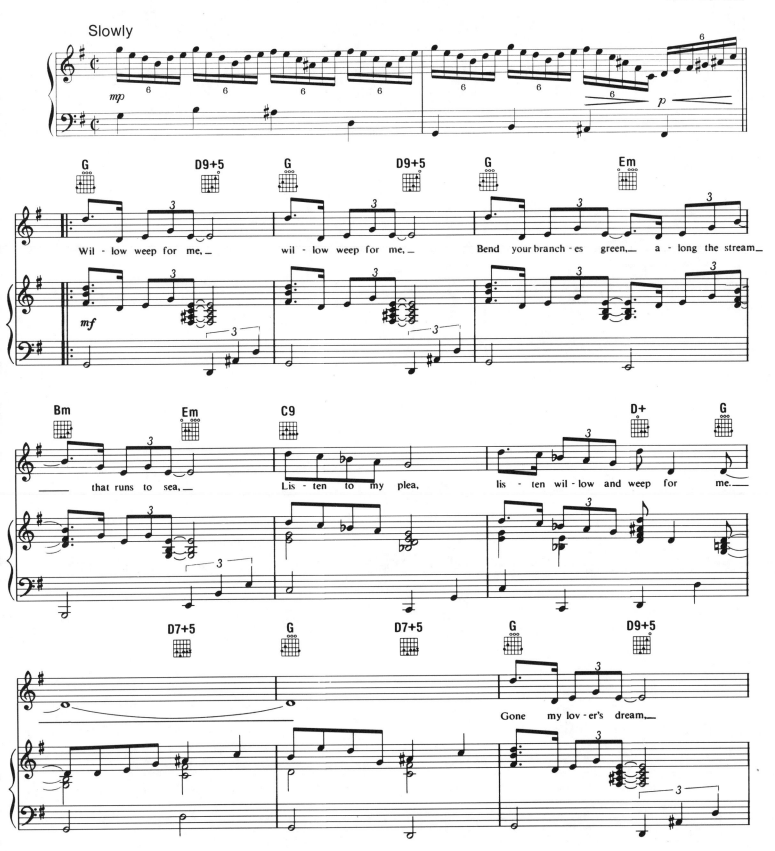

# YOU DON'T KNOW WHAT LOVE IS

Words and Music by DON RAYE
and GENE DePAUL

# WOMAN ALONE WITH THE BLUES

Words and Music by
WILLARD ROBISON